Turn-to-Learn Wheels in Color!
WORD FAMILIES

By Liza Charlesworth

NEW YORK • TORONTO • LONDON • AUCKLAND • SYDNEY
MEXICO CITY • NEW DELHI • HONG KONG • BUENOS AIRES

Teaching *Resources*

Previously published as *Turn-to-Learn Word Family Wheels*

Cover and interior illustrations by Rusty Fletcher
Cover and interior design by Jason Robinson

ISBN : 978-0-545-15433-8

Contents

Word Family Wheels

About This Book

Welcome to *Turn-to-Learn Wheels in Color! Word Families*. The 25 irresistible, interactive wheels in this book were developed to delight and engage children and help put every child in your class on the path to reading success.

Research shows that knowledge of rhyming word families is an essential part of a balanced reading program. When children have repeated encounters with rhyming word families—also known as phonograms—they come to recognize spelling patterns, gaining the ability to decode "member" words by analogy. The ability to decode by analogy is an empowering tool because it enables children to read hundreds and hundreds of words with greater confidence and fluency.

The bright colors, adorable pictures, and playful, guessing-game format invite children to use the wheels over and over, helping them get lots of practice reading words in the same word family. The wheels are also self-correcting, so they provide instant feedback. If a child does miss a word, a turn of the wheel provides a fresh opportunity to try again. In addition, the wheels will help children meet key language arts standards. (See page 10 for more information.)

You can use the wheels as the focus of a one-on-one lesson, place them in a learning center for children to use independently or in pairs, and even make multiple copies of each wheel for greater flexibility. (See "Using the CD," page 6, for more.) However you choose to incorporate the wheels in your classroom routine, children will enjoy this playful spin on reading instruction!

Assembling the Word Family Wheels

WHAT YOU NEED

- scissors
- brass fastener
- craft knife (adult use only)

WHAT TO DO

1. Each wheel consists of two parts: a window wheel and a picture wheel. Remove the pages for each wheel from the book. (If you like, glue the pages to cardstock and/or laminate them for added durability.) Then cut out both wheels along the outer solid lines.

2. Place the window wheel on a protected surface. Then use a craft knife to cut out the word window and the picture-window flap along the dashed lines.

3. Place the window wheel on top of the picture wheel. Insert a brass fastener through the crosses at the center as shown below, and open the prongs on the back to secure.

Window Wheel   +   Picture Wheel   =   Completed Wheel

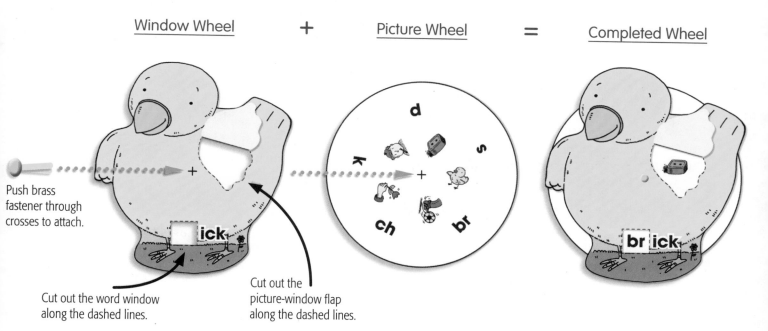

Push brass fastener through crosses to attach.

Cut out the word window along the dashed lines.

Cut out the picture-window flap along the dashed lines.

Introducing the Word Family Wheels

1. Show children a sample wheel, for example, the wheel for –*ake*. Invite them to identify the picture on the window wheel (a *cake*), and think about the sound at the end of this word. Then point out the –*ake* word family on the window wheel and read it aloud.

2. Show children how to turn the picture wheel so that the onset letter *c* appears in the window and lines up with the –*ake* word family. Encourage children to sound out the word *cake* aloud. They can then open the flap door and see if they read the word correctly by checking the picture cue.

3. Let children turn the wheel to form and then read a new word, for example, *rake*. Ask: "What do you notice about this word?" (*It rhymes with* cake, *contains the same* –ake *word family, begins with a different letter.*)

4. Invite children to turn the wheel and practice sounding out each of the five words. Repeated practice will help children master each word and build automaticity. (See page 7 for quick-and-easy activities to extend learning.)

Creating Customized Wheels

Make additional wheels to help children practice other words in each of the featured word families in the book. You'll find a list on each picture wheel page.

● Use the CD to print a copy of the window wheel for a target word family (in color or black and white) and a blank picture wheel. Cut out and assemble the wheel.

● Use the list of words from the picture wheel page, or invite children to suggest other "picturable" words that contain the same word family, and draw or find pictures to illustrate each word.

● To help children explore other key word families, use the word lists on page 9 to create additional wheels.

Tip

The wheels work best if children turn the bottom wheel while holding the top wheel in place.

Using the CD

The CD that comes with this book includes ready-to-print versions of each of the 25 word family wheels in both full-color and black-line formats. It also includes blank templates for creating customized wheels. Make extra wheels to create class sets, to place in a learning center for small groups of children to explore independently, or to tuck inside backpacks to build at-home literacy.

Activities to Extend Learning

Give children additional opportunities to explore word families either before introducing the wheels or after. Here are some suggestions.

Super Silly Sentences

Choose a word family such as -at. With children, brainstorm a long list of rhyming words (*flat, mat, that, sat, rat, cat, hat, fat*). Write them on the board or on cards that can be reordered on the chalk/eraser tray. Next, challenge children to work together to make up a sentence that includes as many of the words as possible; for example: *The fat cat that sat on the mat wanted to wear the rat's flat hat.* Let children know that sentences can get super silly! For added fun, ask volunteers to illustrate one or more of the sentences.

Beanbag Rhyme Toss

Support kinesthetic learners with this engaging rhyming game. Invite children to stand in a circle and toss a beanbag around. Start them off with a word family that is easy to rhyme, such as *bug*. Invite the child holding the beanbag to name a rhyming word (for example, *hug*) and then toss it to the child to his or her right to do the same. If a child cannot name a new rhyming word, he or she says "pass" and hands—not tosses—the beanbag to the next child. When three children in a row say "pass," it's time to start a new game with a fresh word family.

Collaborative Word-Family Dictionaries

Enrich learning by publishing a class set of word-family dictionaries. Divide the class into cooperative groups and assign each a different word family (-ill, -ink, -unk, and so on). Challenge each group of book-makers to work together to write a new rhyming word on every page, illustrate them with simple pictures, and then label the cover (for example, "Our -ail Words"). When the books are complete, place them in an accessible spot for children to turn to for friendly reading, writing, and spelling support.

Rhyme-Time Concentration

Using two or more word family lists for reference, jot rhyming words on index cards—one word to each card. (Make sure to include an even number of rhyming words in each family.) Shuffle the cards, then place them facedown in rows. Invite children to take turns turning over the cards to make matches. If two words rhyme (such as *ban* and *van*), the child gets to keep the cards and try again. Play continues until all of the cards have been picked up; the child with the most cards wins the game.

Go Fish-Dish-Wish!

Make a class set of about 36 playing cards, using several different rhyming word pairs. (You can purchase blank playing cards at many teacher stores.) Tell children that they will be using the cards to play "Go Fish-Dish-Wish." The rules of the game are the same as classic "Go Fish," except children will be looking for sets of rhyming words instead of numbers/face cards. The child with the most matches wins the game.

Clap and Stamp Poetry

Read aloud lots and lots of poems! Some great sources include *The Big Book of Pocket Chart Poems: ABCs & 123s*, *A Poem a Day*, *Poem of the Week*, *The Super Book of Phonics Poems*, and *70 Wonderful Word Family Poems* (all from Scholastic Teaching Resources). As you read a poem, invite children to clap and stamp each time they hear a rhyming word. (For a greater challenger, assign a different action for each new word family.) This activity is a great—and meaningful—way to "shake out the sillies" during circle time.

"I Spy" Rhymes

Play a rhyming word version of "I Spy," using items in your classroom. For example, "I spy with my little eye, something that rhymes with *cap*." (*map*) Or "I spy with my little eye, something that rhymes with *clock*." (*smock*) Once children have mastered the concept, invite them to generate their own riddles to share with classmates.

Rhyming Relay Race

Divide the class into three or four teams, and have each line up. On the board, write a different word for each team—for example, *cake*, *hill*, and *duck*. (Make sure to select word families with lots of rhyming possibilities.) Next, challenge each child, in turn, to come up to the board and add a rhyming word to his or her team's list. Team members can help each other out. The team that generates the longest list wins!

Word Lists for Other Key Word Families

-ack	-ash	-eat	-ine	-oke	-ot
hack	bash	beat	dine	coke	cot
Jack	cash	feat	line	joke	dot
lack	dash	heat	mine	poke	got
Mack	gash	meat	nine	woke	hot
pack	hash	neat	vine	yoke	jot
quack	lash	seat	shine	broke	lot
rack	mash		shrine	chock	not
tack	rash	**-ice**	twine	smoke	rot
black	brash	dice	whine	stoke	tot
clack	clash	lice		stroke	blot
crack	flash	mice	**-it**		clot
knack	slash	nice	bit	**-ore**	knot
shack	smash	rice	fit	bore	plot
slack	stash	price	hit	core	shot
smack	thrash	slice	kit	lore	slot
snack	trash	splice	lit	more	spot
stack			pit	pore	trot
track	**-aw**	**-in**	quit	sore	
whack	law	fin	sit	wore	
	paw	kin	wit	chore	
-ame	raw	pin	flit	shore	
came	claw	win	grit	snore	
dame	draw	chin	skit	store	
fame	slaw	grin	slit		
game	straw	shin	spit		
lame	thaw	spin	split		
name					
tame					
blame					
flame					
frame					
shame					

Meeting the Language Arts Standards

Connections to the McREL Language Arts Standards

Mid-continent Research for Education and Learning (McREL), a nationally recognized nonprofit organization, has compiled and evaluated national and state standards—and proposed what teachers should provide for their PreK–K students to grow proficient in language arts. This book's activities support the following standards:

Uses the general skills and strategies of the reading process including:

- Knows uppercase and lowercase letters of the alphabet
- Uses basic elements of phonetic analysis (e.g., understands sound-symbol relationships; beginning and ending consonants, vowel sounds) to decode unknown words

Uses grammatical and mechanical conventions in written compositions including:

- Uses conventions of print in writing (e.g., forms letters in print, uses uppercase and lowercase letters of the alphabet)

Source: Kendall, J. S. & Marzano, R. J. (2004). *Content knowledge: A compendium of standards and benchmarks for K–12 education*. Aurora, CO: Mid-continent Research for Education and Learning Online database: http://www.mcrel.org/standards-benchmarks/

Connections to Early Childhood Language Arts Standards

The activities in this book are also designed to support you in meeting the following PreK–K literacy goals and recommendations established in a joint position statement by the International Reading Association (IRA) and the National Association for the Education of Young Children (NAEYC):

- Understands that print carries a message
- Engages in reading and writing attempts
- Recognizes letters and letter-sound matches
- Begins to write

Source: *Learning to Read and Write: Developmentally Appropriate Practices for Young Children*, a joint position statement of the International Reading Association (IRA) and the National Association for the Education of Young Children (NAEYC). http://www.naeyc.org/about/positions/pdf/PSREAD98.PDF © 1998 by the National Association for the Education of Young Children

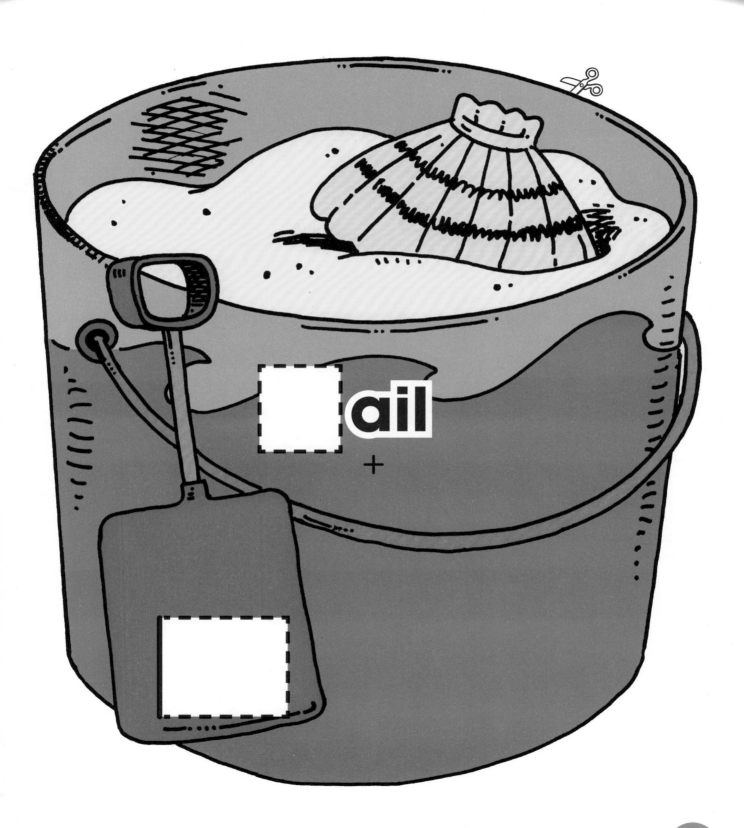

ail

+

Word Family: -ail

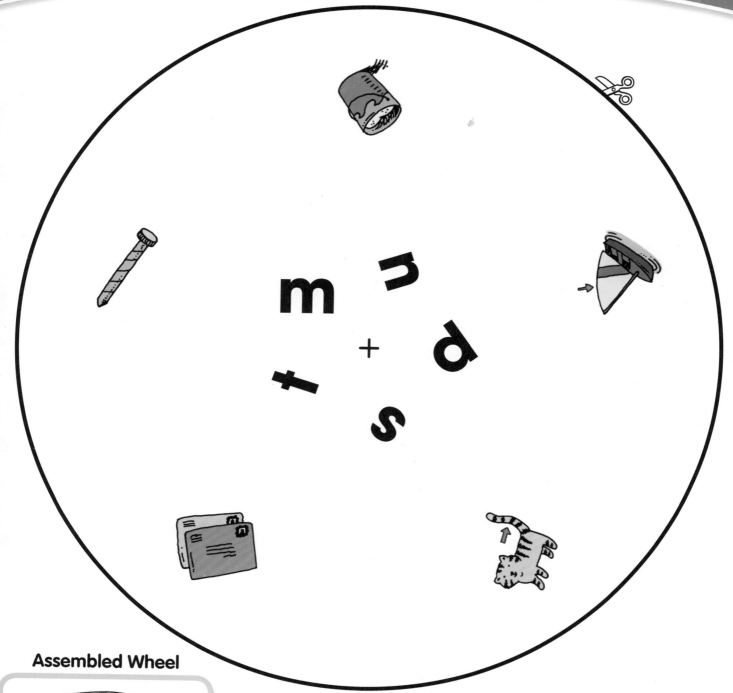

Assembled Wheel

More -ail Words

bail	hail	rail	frail
fail	jail	wail	snail
Gail	quail	flail	trail

Word Family: -ain

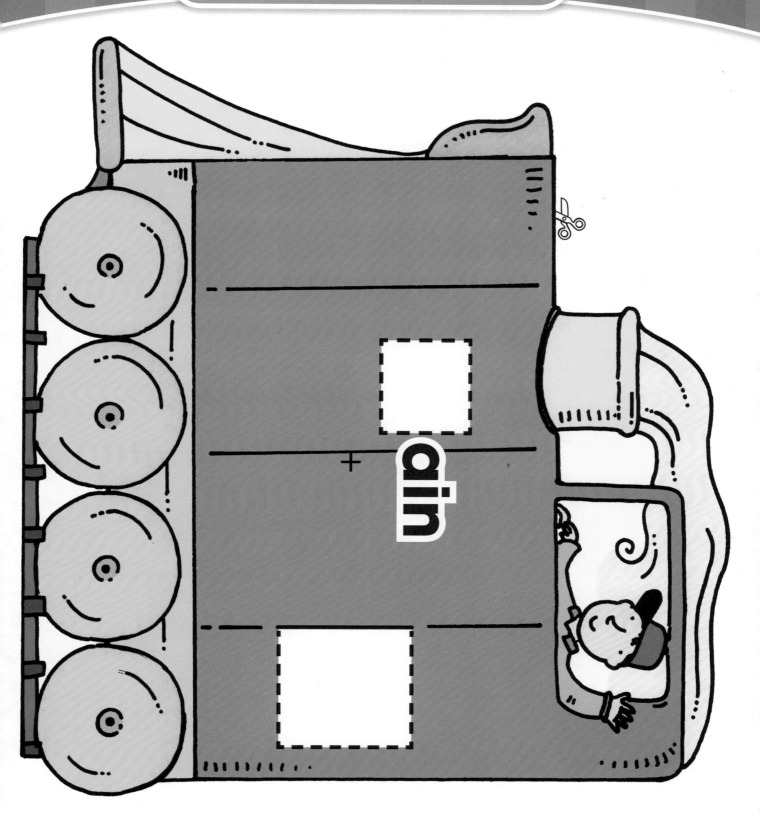

Word Family: -ain

Assembled Wheel

More -ain Words

gain	vain	Spain
main	grain	stain
pain	plain	strain

ake

Word Family: -ake

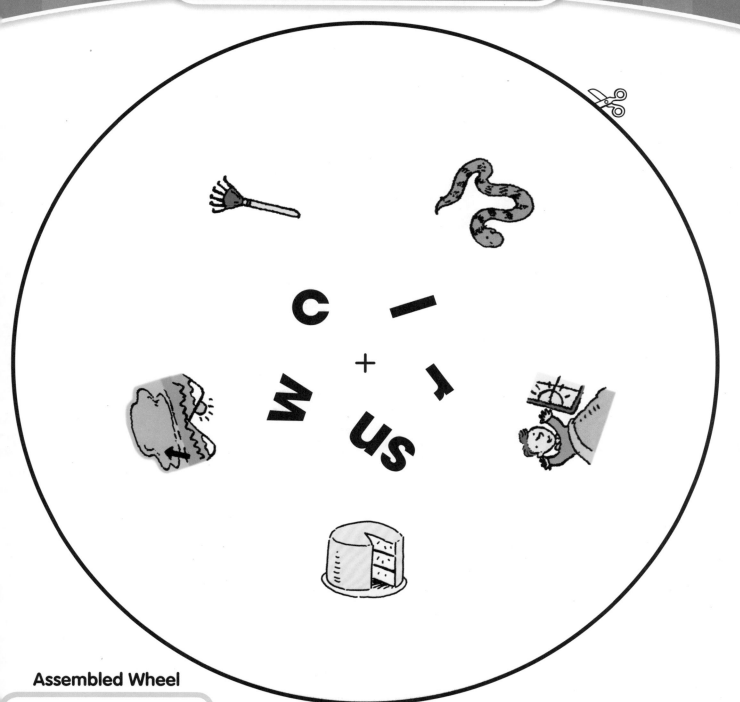

Assembled Wheel

r ake

More -ake Words

bake	make	take	flake
fake	quake	brake	shake
Jake	sake	drake	stake

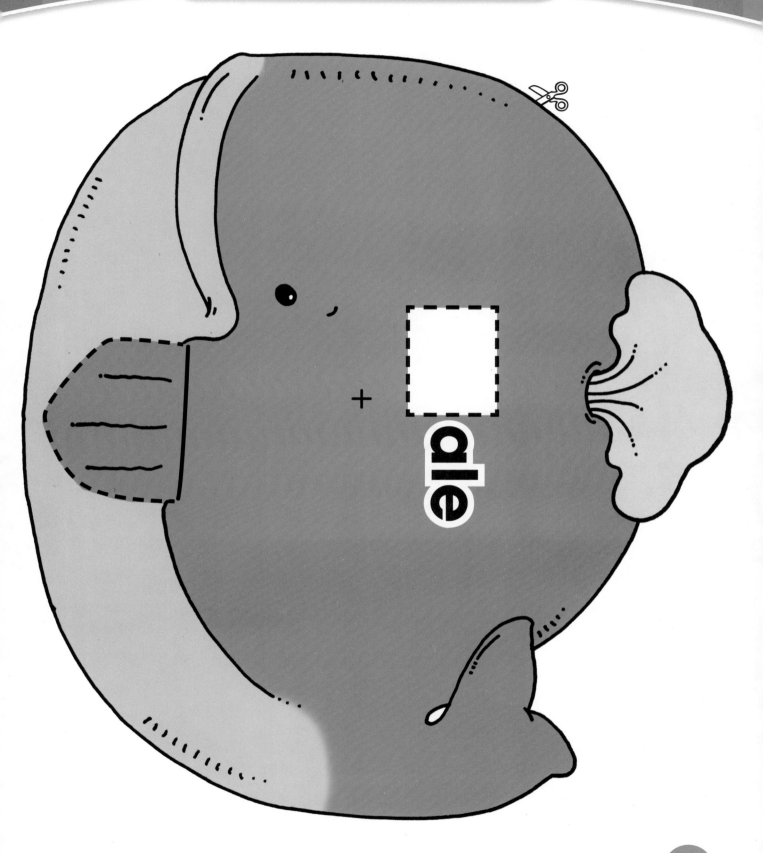

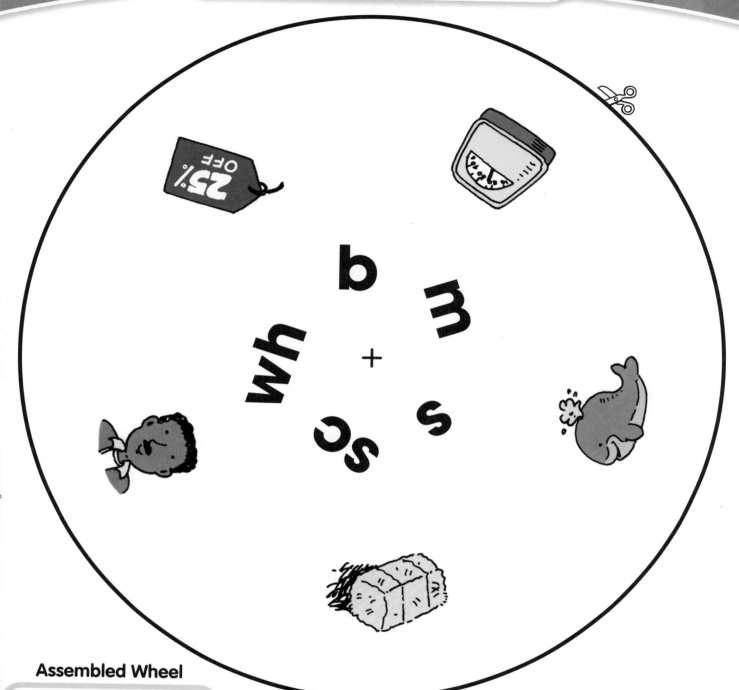

Assembled Wheel

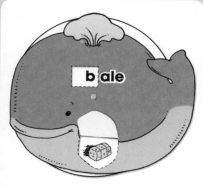

b ale

More -ale Words

Dale	pale	stale
gale	tale	

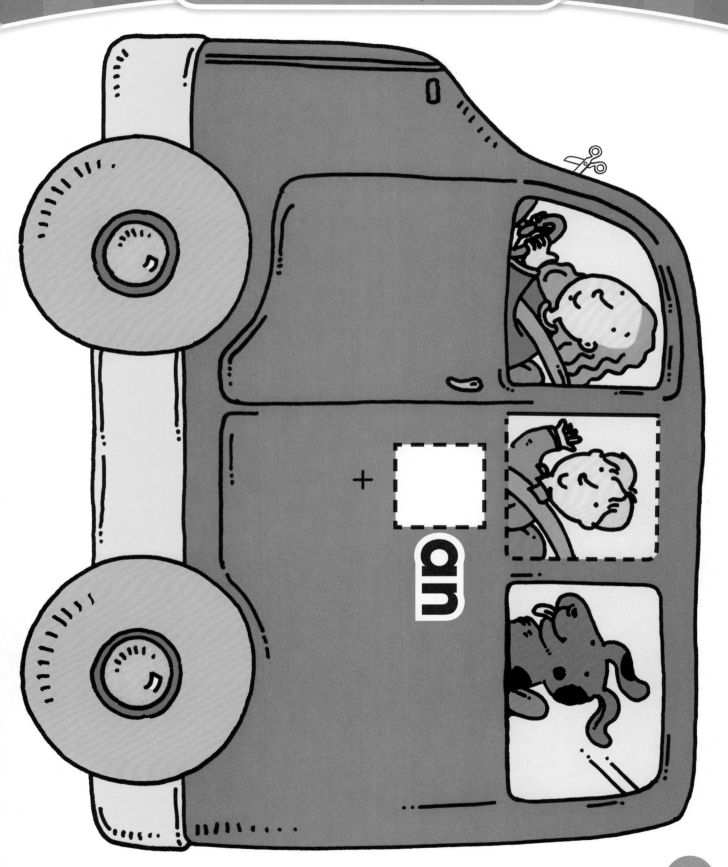

Word Family: -an

Assembled Wheel

More -an Words

ban	ran	clan	spam
Dan	tan	plan	Stan
Jan	bran	scan	than

29

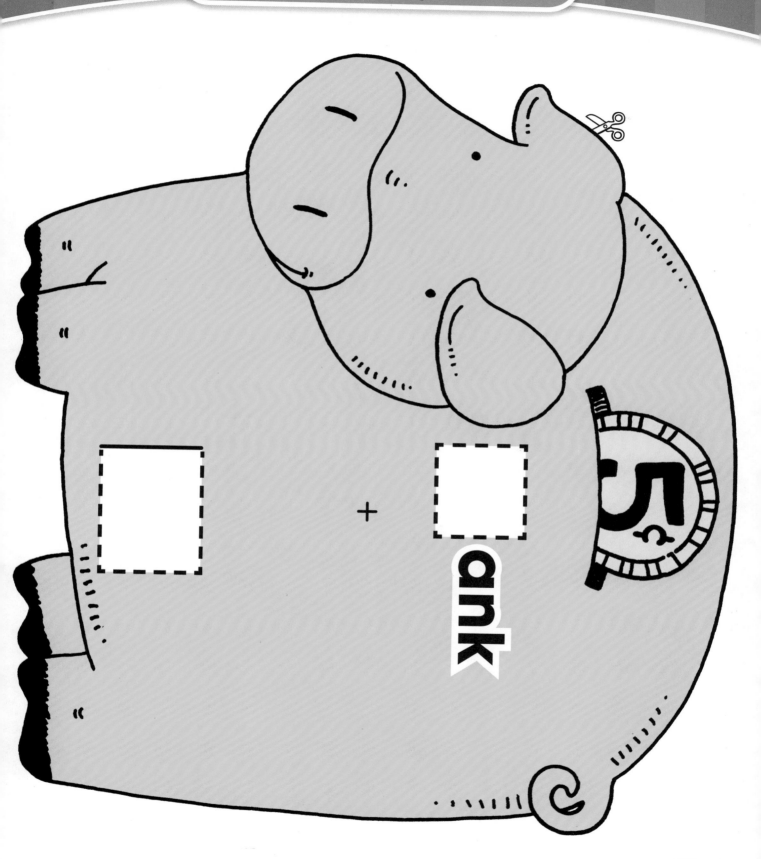

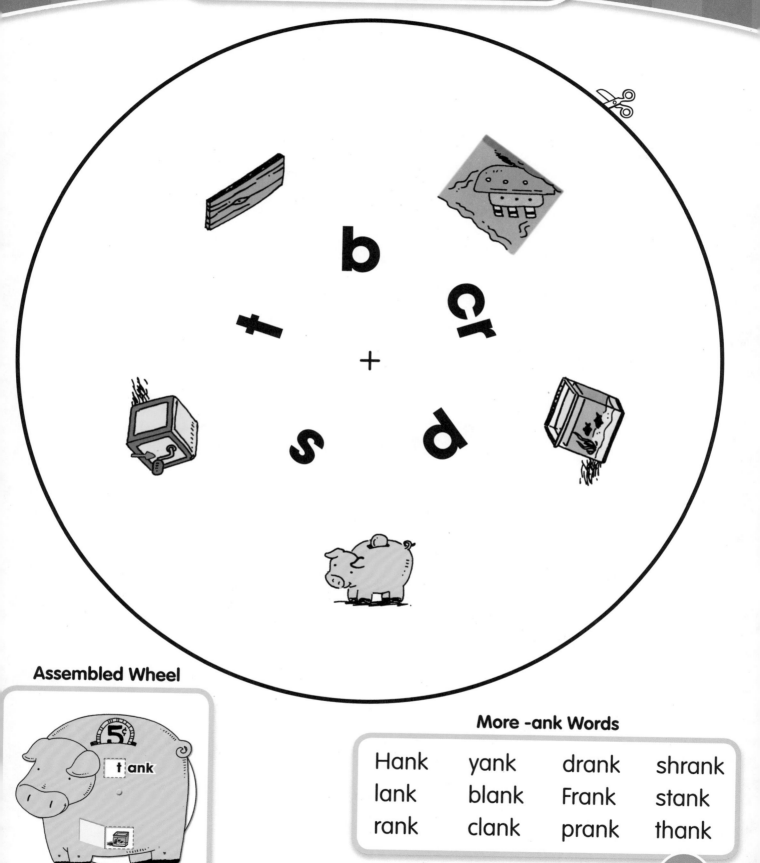

Assembled Wheel

More -ank Words

Hank	yank	drank	shrank
lank	blank	Frank	stank
rank	clank	prank	thank

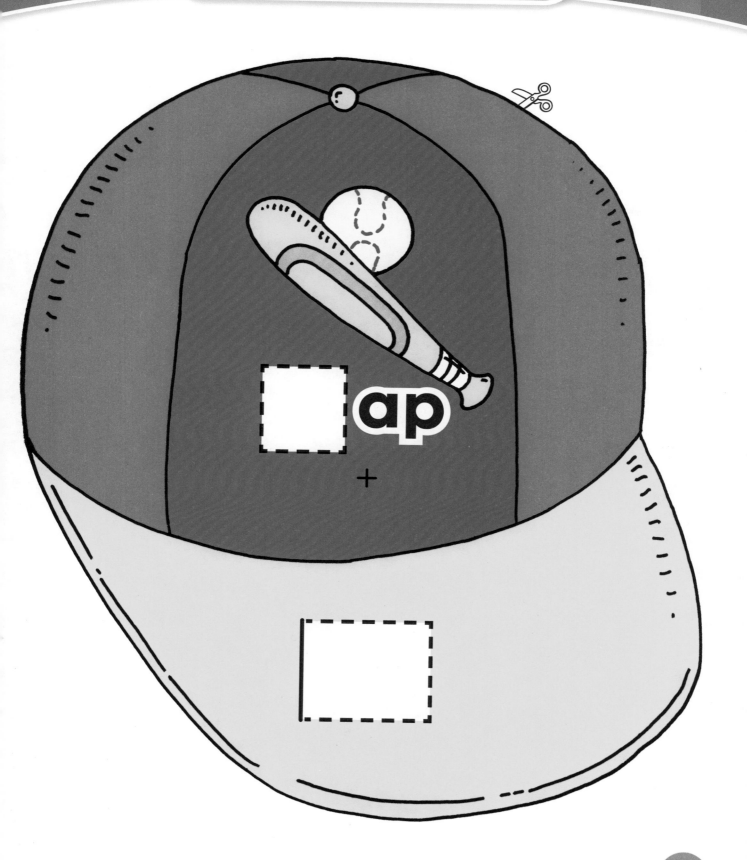

ap

Word Family: -ap

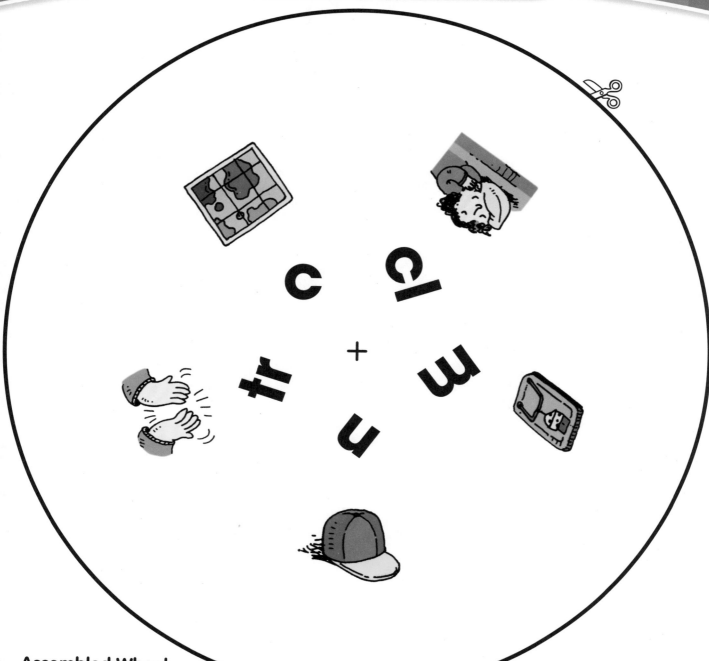

Assembled Wheel

More -ap Words

gap	sap	flap	snap
lap	tap	scrap	strap
rap	yap	slap	wrap

at

Word Family: -at

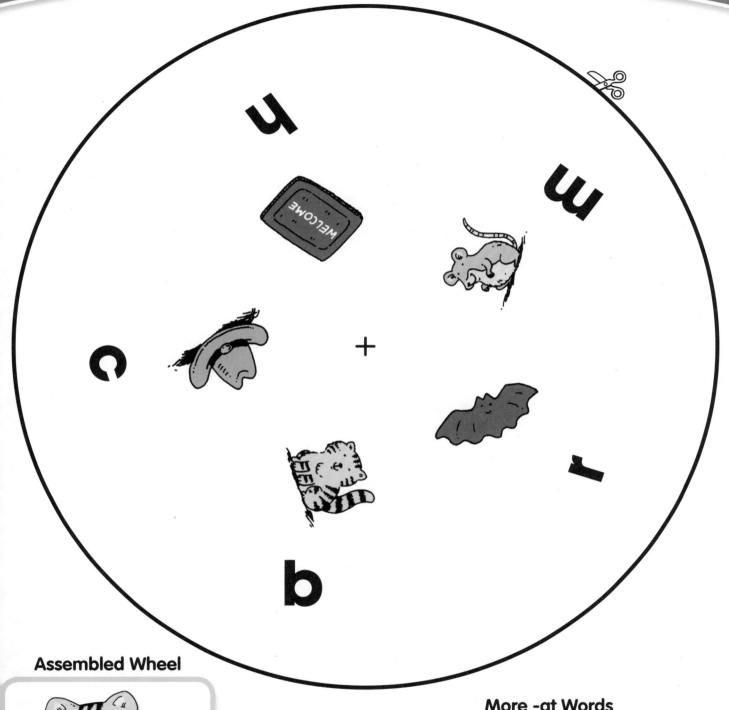

Assembled Wheel

More -at Words

fat	sat	chat	slat
gnat	vat	flat	spat
pat	brat	scat	that

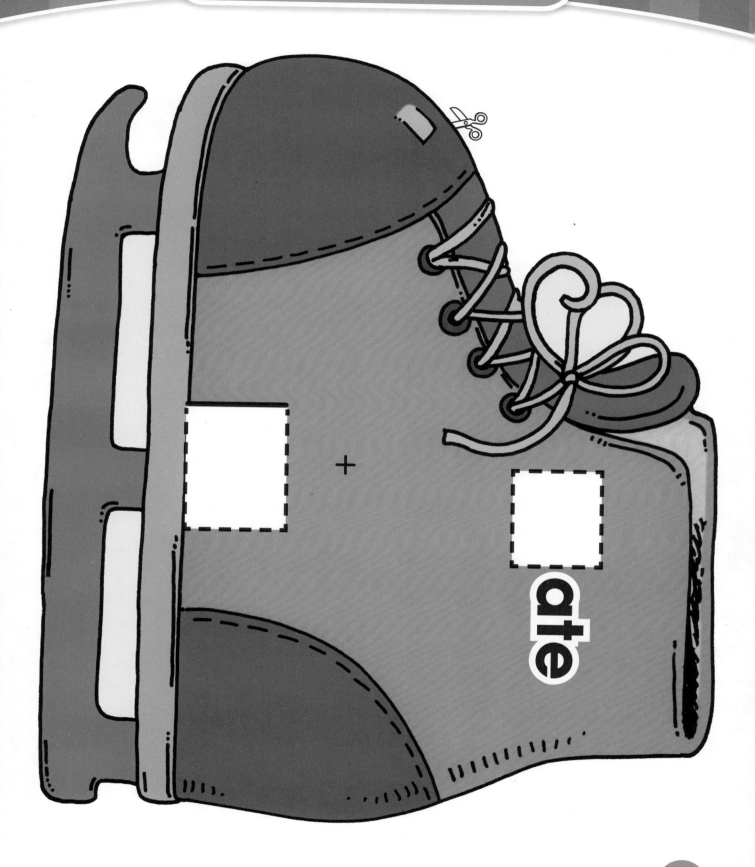

Word Family: -ate

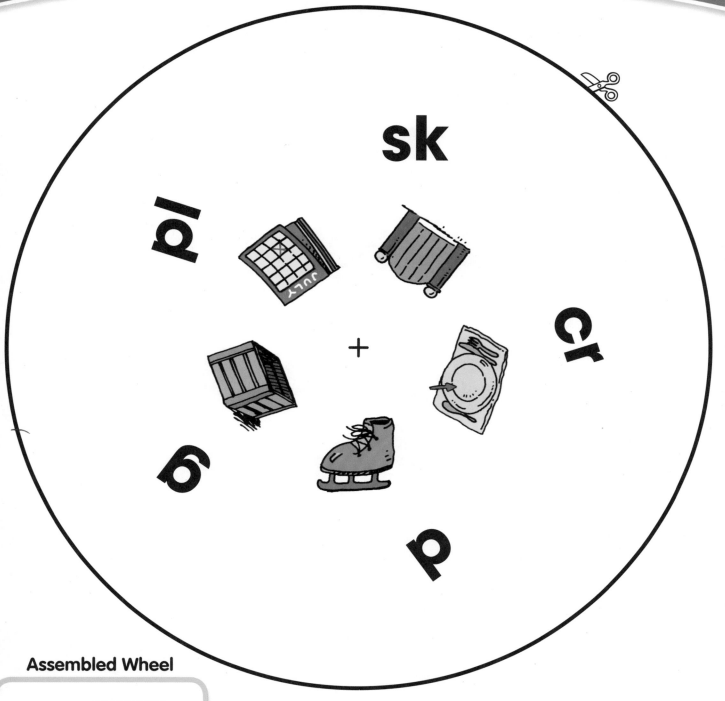

Assembled Wheel

d ate

More -ate Words

ate	hate	late	Nate	grate
fate	Kate	mate	rate	state

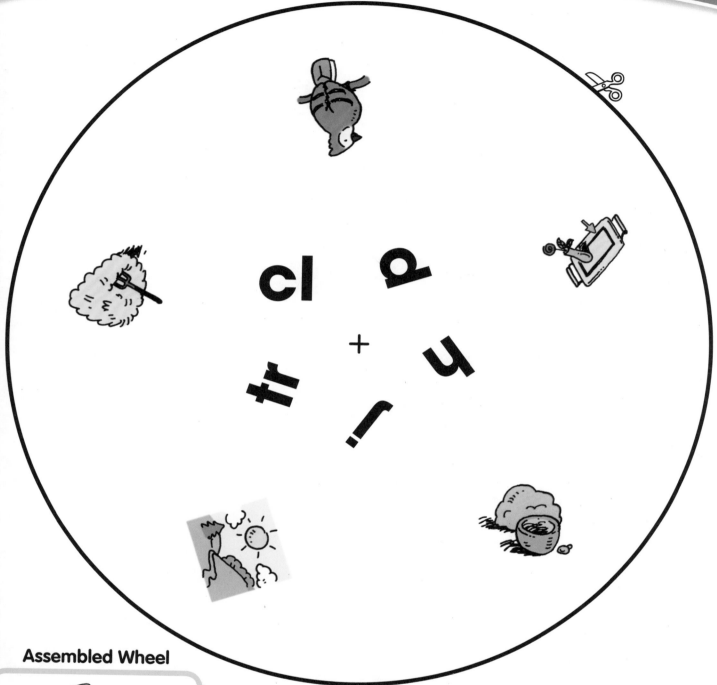

Assembled Wheel

More -ay Words

bay	may	say	gray	slay	stray
gay	pay	way	play	spray	sway
lay	ray	fray	pray	stay	

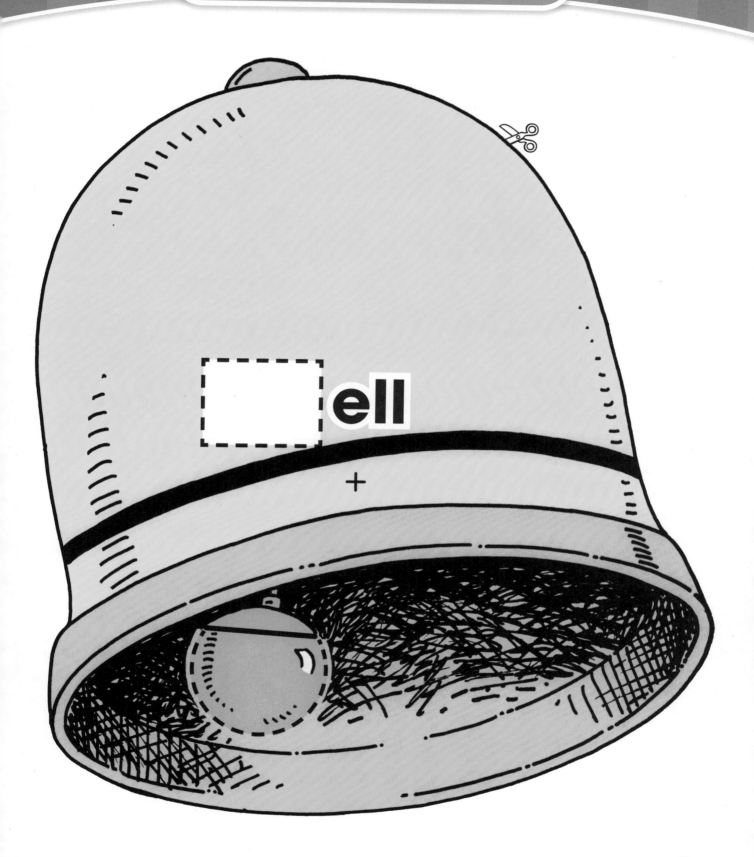

ell

+

Word Family: -ell

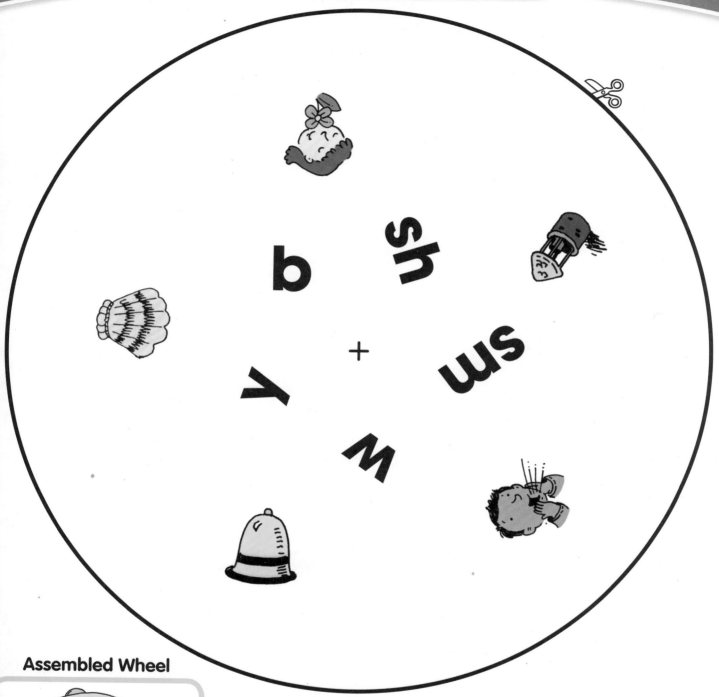

Assembled Wheel

sh ell

More -ell Words

| cell | fell | Nell | tell | spell |
| dell | jell | sell | dwell | swell |

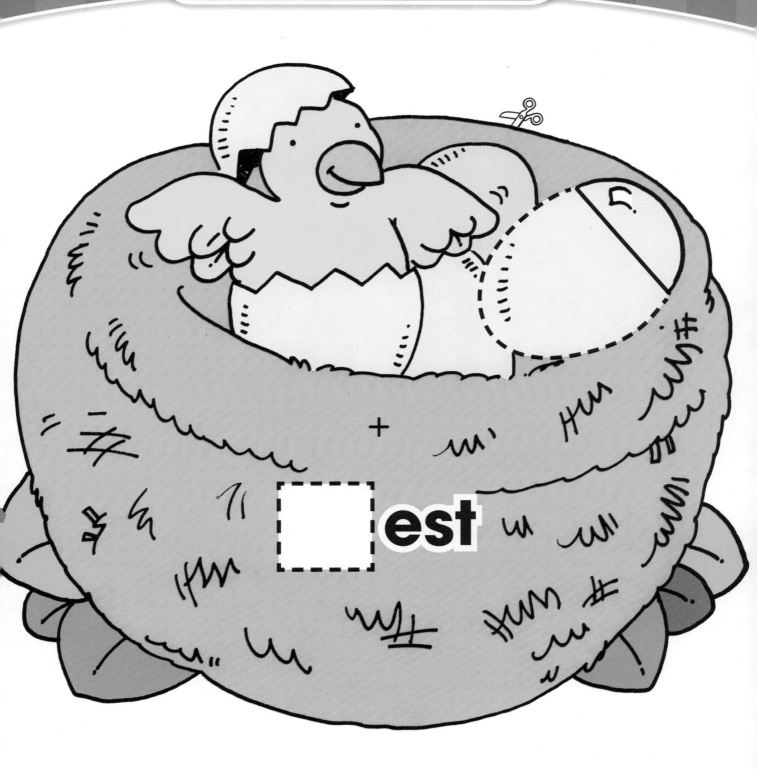

est

Word Family: -est

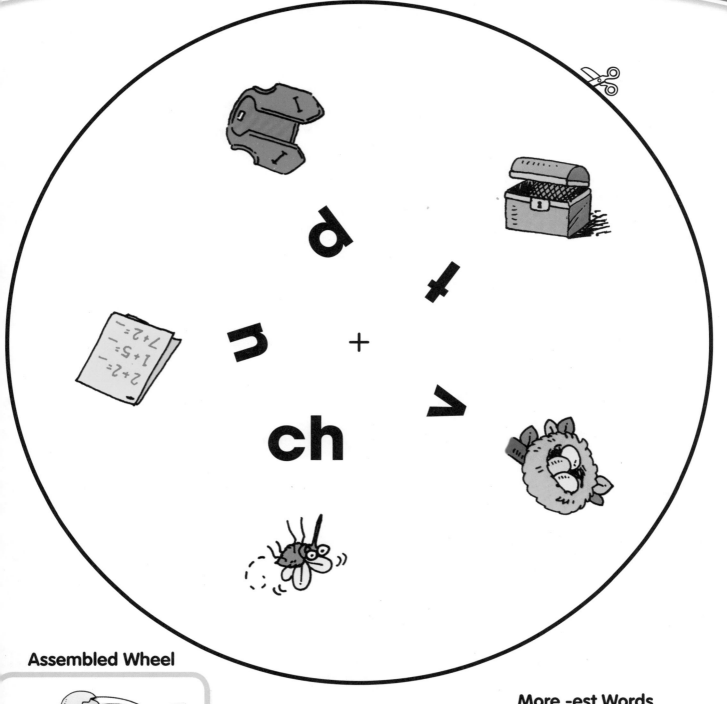

Assembled Wheel

ch est

More -est Words

best	rest	crest
guest	west	quest
jest	zest	

ick

Word Family: -ick

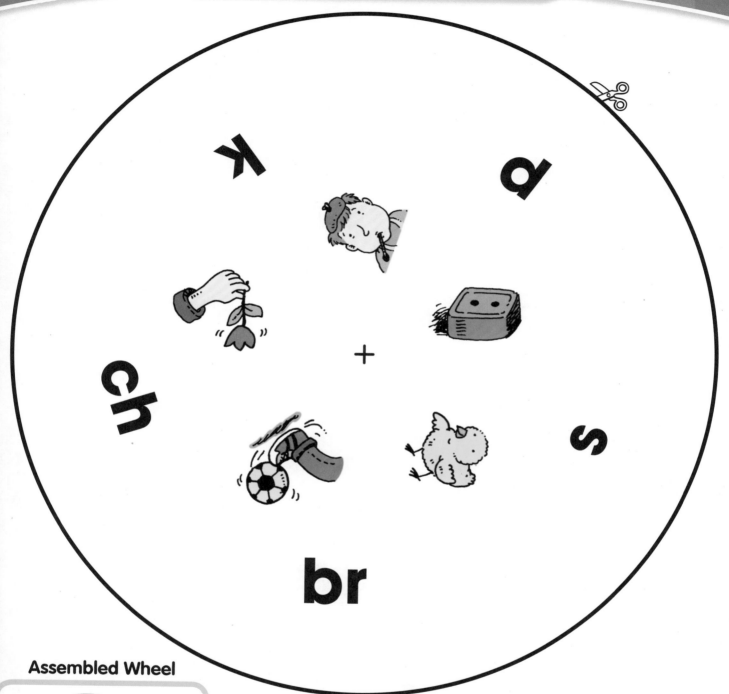

Assembled Wheel

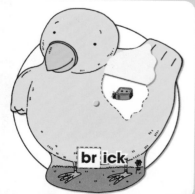

More -ick Words

Dick	quick	click	stick
lick	tick	flick	thick
Nick	wick	slick	trick

Word Family: -ide

ide

Word Family: -ide

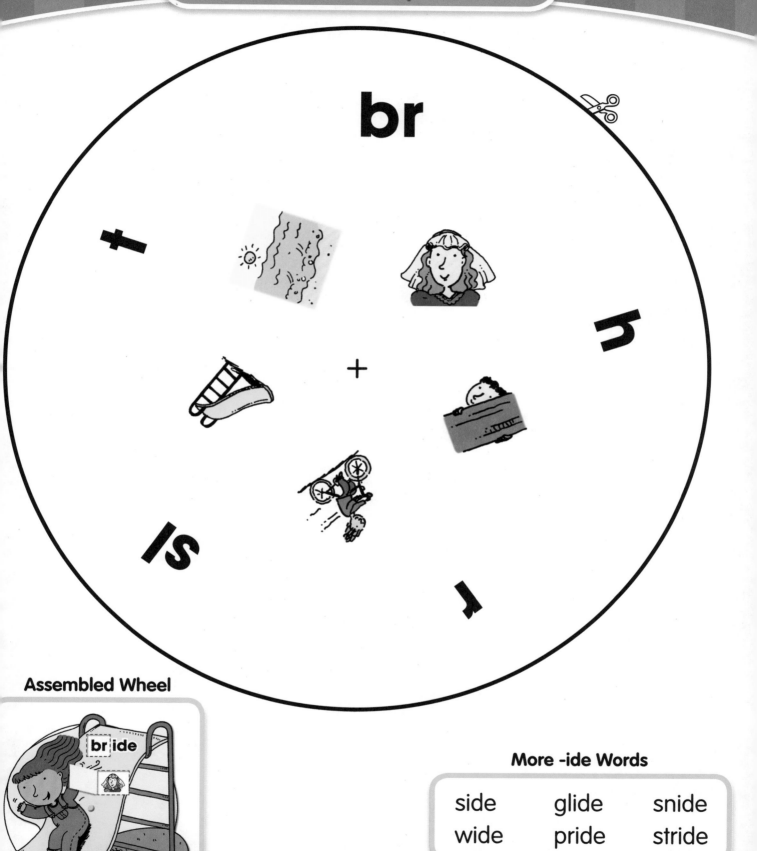

br

t

h

sl

r

+

Assembled Wheel

br ide

More -ide Words

side	glide	snide
wide	pride	stride

ight

+

Word Family: -ight

Assembled Wheel

More -ight Words

might	tight	fright
right	blight	plight
sight	bright	slight

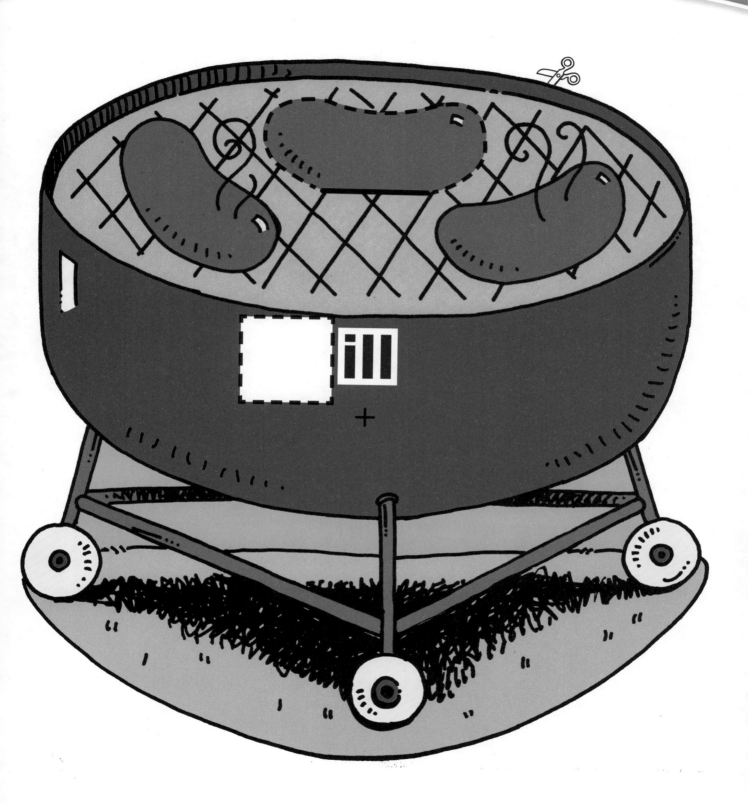

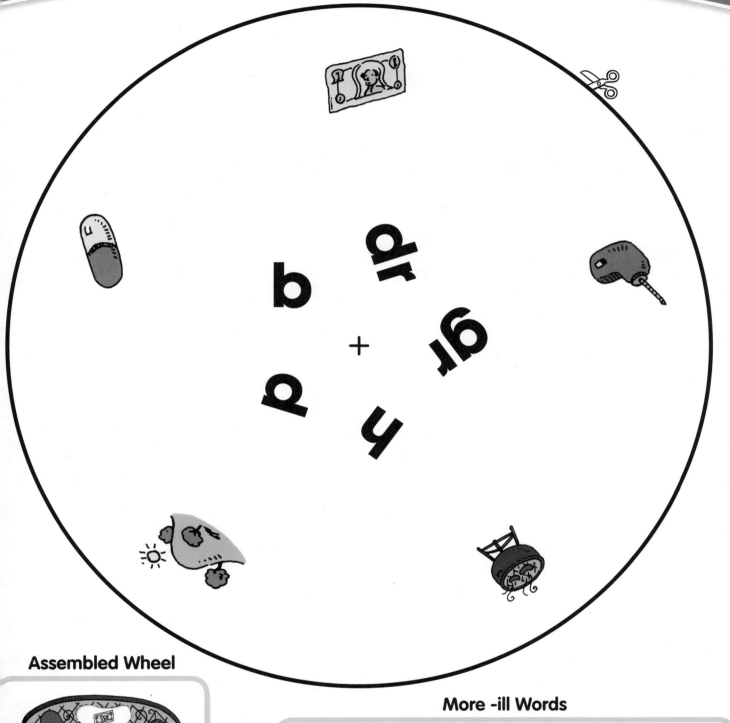

Assembled Wheel

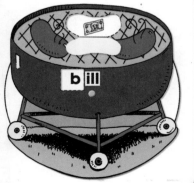

More -ill Words

dill	ill	mill	till	frill	still
fill	Jill	quill	will	skill	thrill
gill	kill	sill	chill	spill	trill

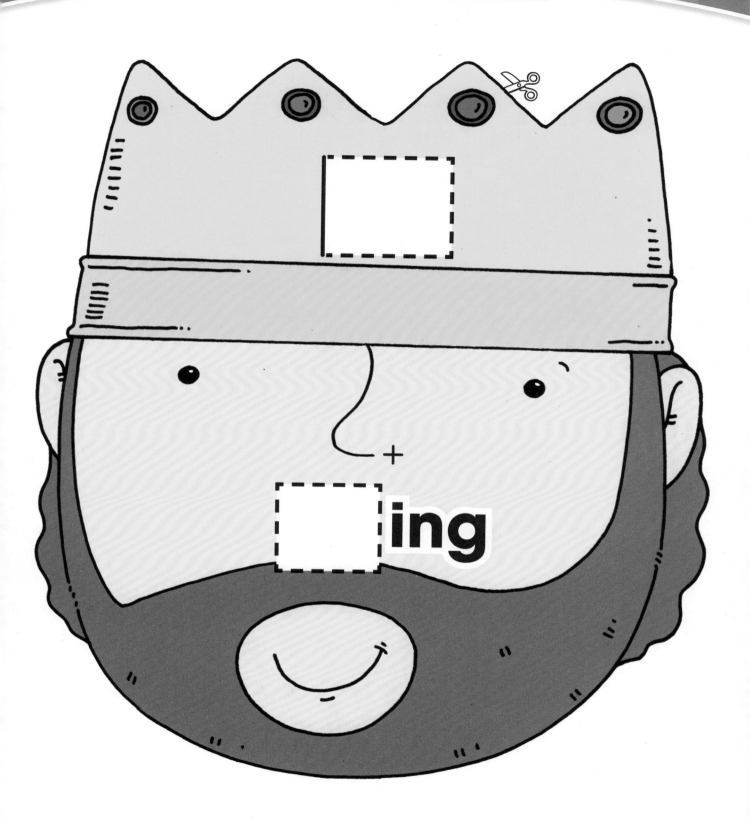

ing

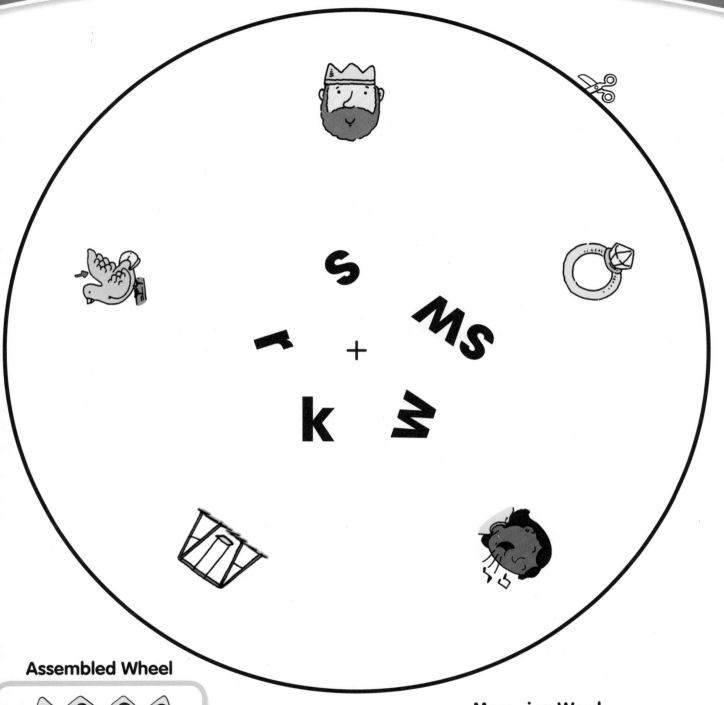

Assembled Wheel

w ing

More -ing Words

bing	zing	fling	string
ding	bring	sling	thing
ping	cling	sting	wring

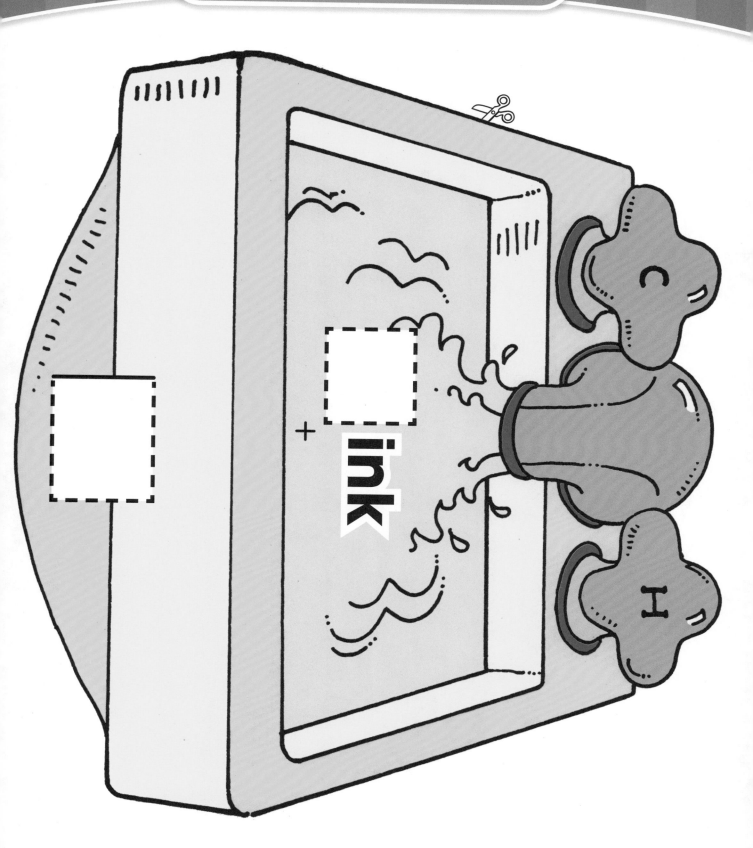

+ **ink**

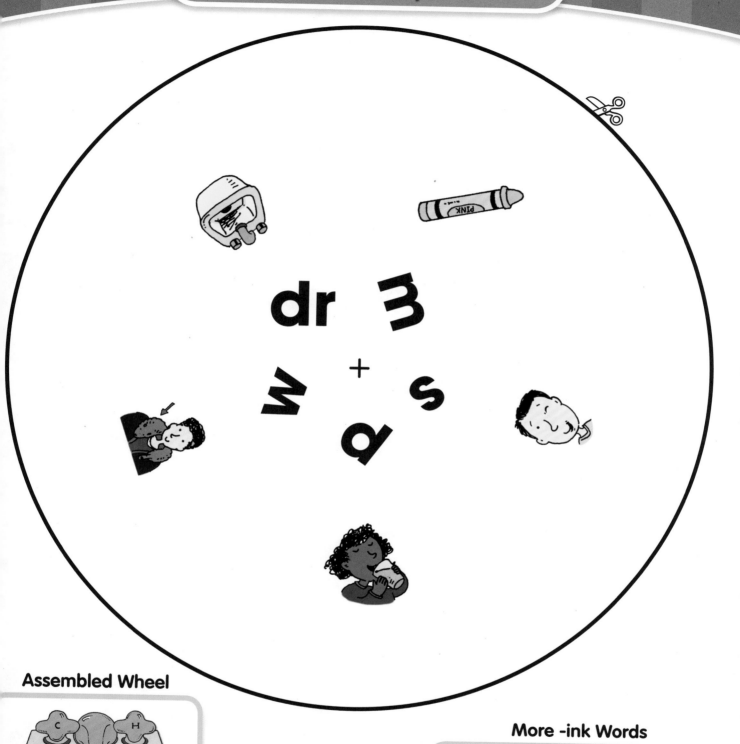

Assembled Wheel

dr ink

More -ink Words

kink	blink	shrink
link	brink	slink
rink	clink	think

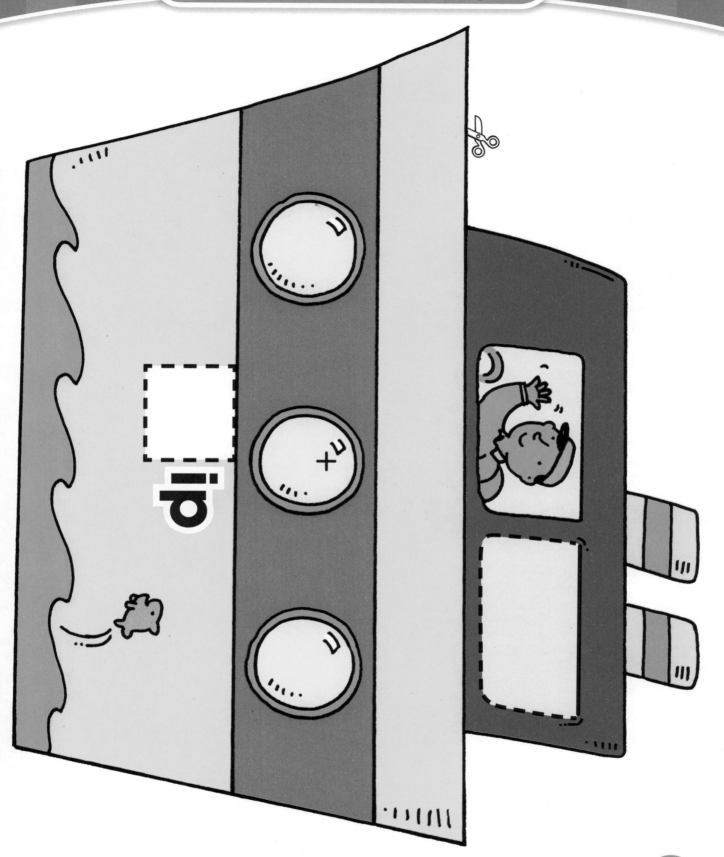

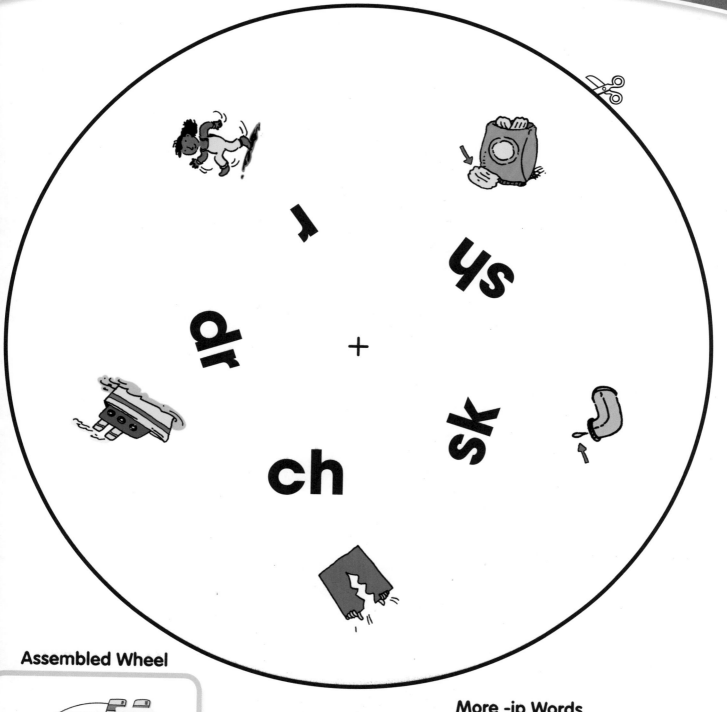

Assembled Wheel

More -ip Words

dip	nip	blip	grip	strip
hip	sip	clip	slip	trip
lip	tip	flip	snip	whip

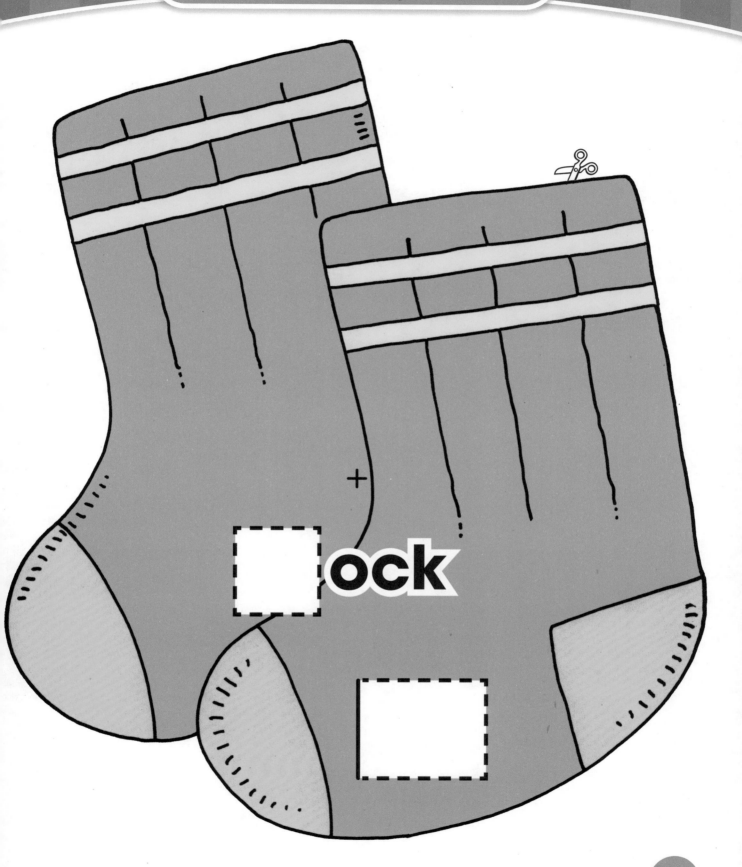

ock

cl p
+
s r

Assembled Wheel

d ock

More -ock Words

mock	crock	shock
tock	flock	smock
block	frock	stock

op

STOP

Word Family: -op

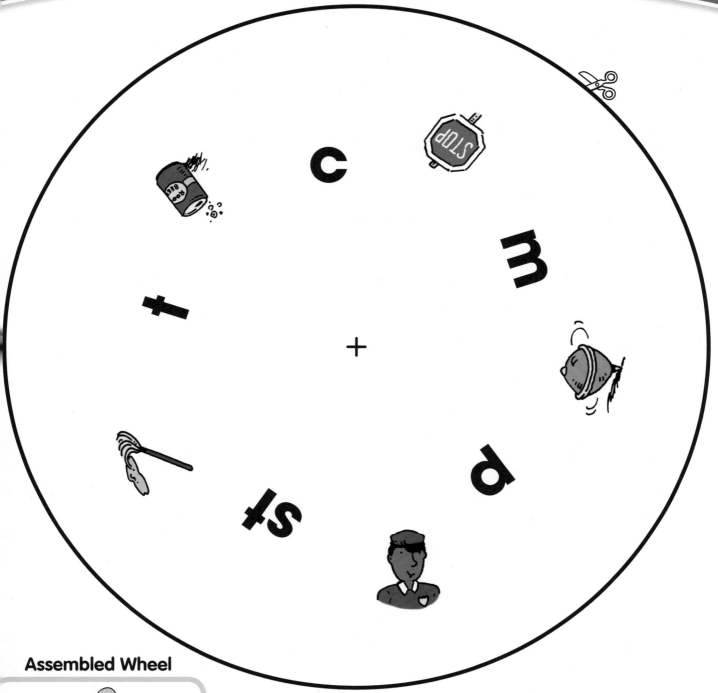

Assembled Wheel

More -op Words

bop	crop	plop
lop	drop	prop
sop	flop	slop

93

uck

+

Word Family: -uck

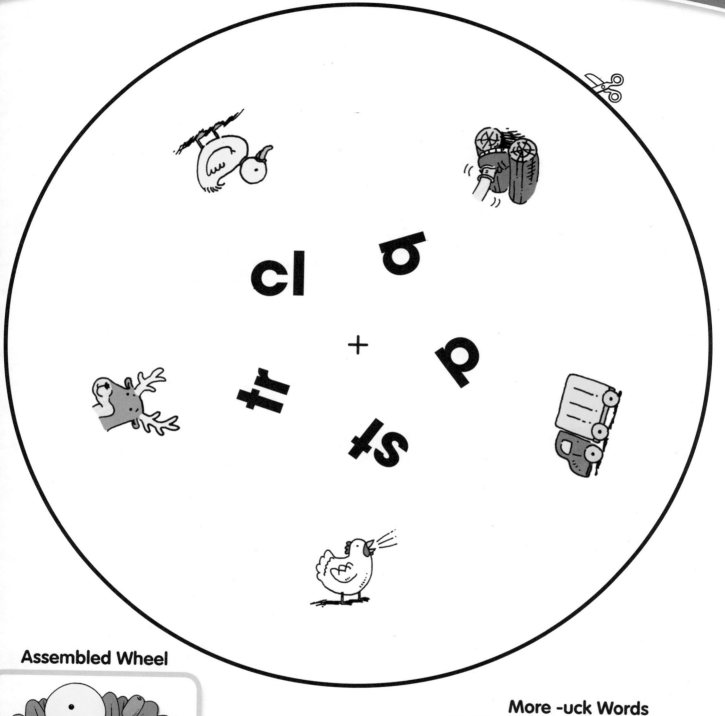

Assembled Wheel

tr|uck

More -uck Words

luck	suck	Chuck
muck	tuck	pluck
puck	yuck	struck

97

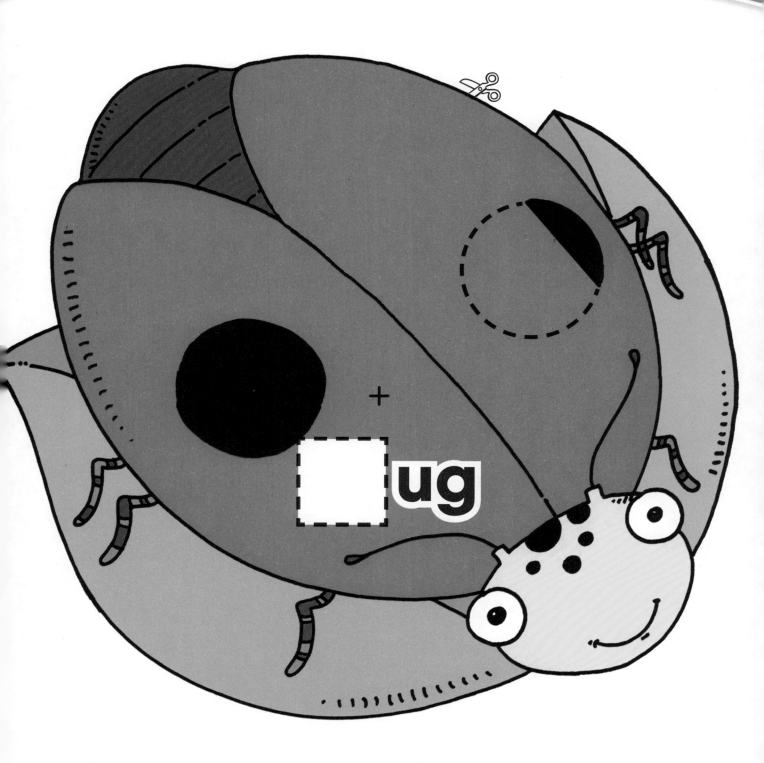

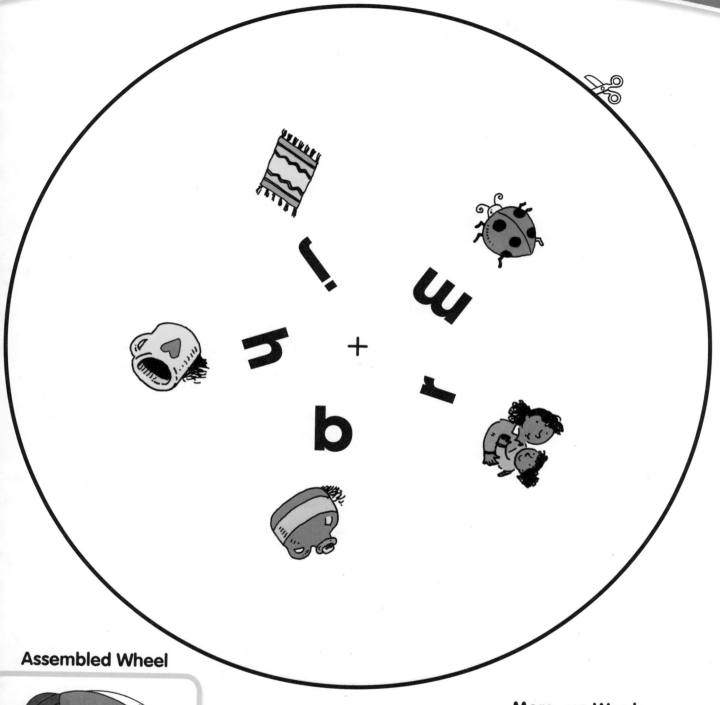

Assembled Wheel

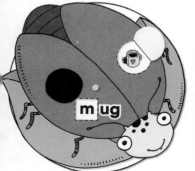

More -ug Words

dug	chug	smug
lug	drug	snug
pug	shrug	thug

ump

+

Word Family: -ump

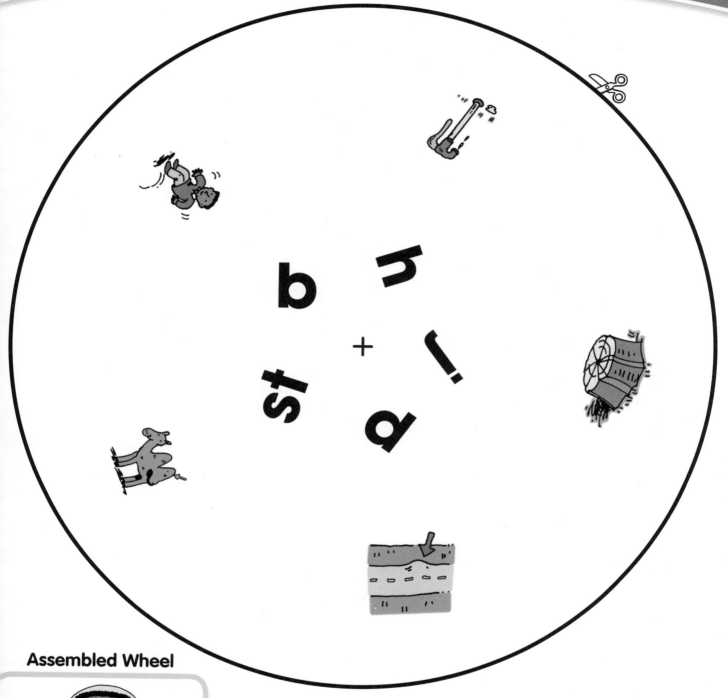

Assembled Wheel

b ump

More -ump Words

dump	clump	plump
lump	frump	slump
chump	grump	thump

105

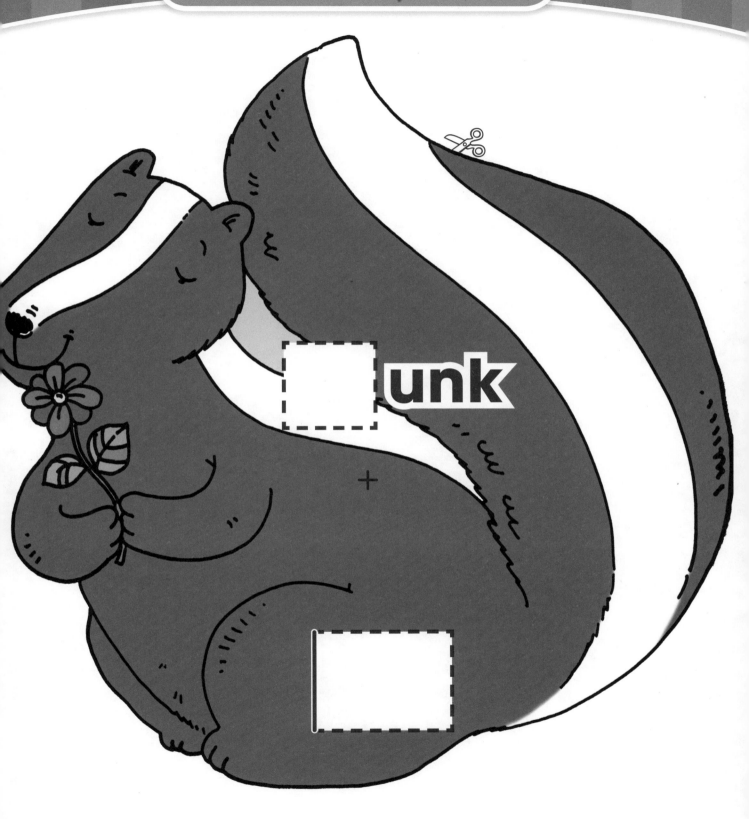

unk

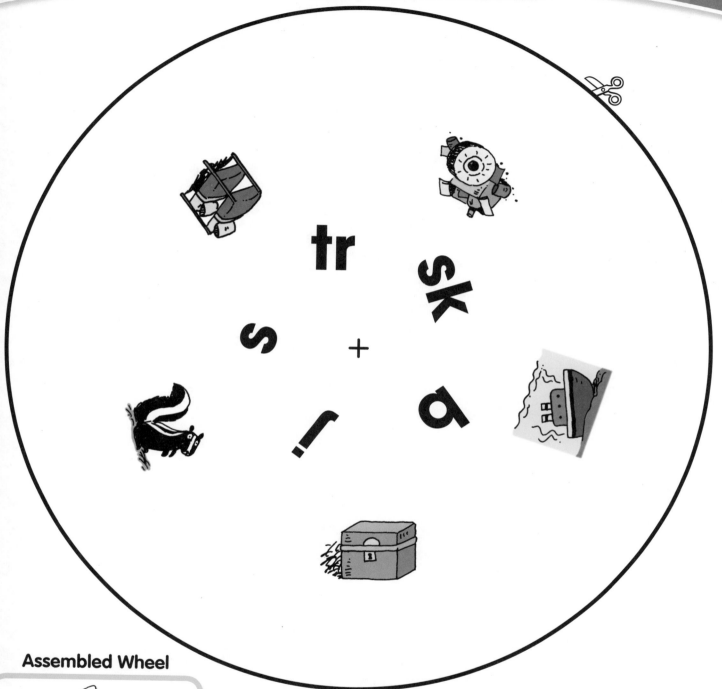

Assembled Wheel

More -unk Words

dunk	chunk	flunk	slunk
hunk	clunk	plunk	spunk
punk	drunk	shrunk	stunk

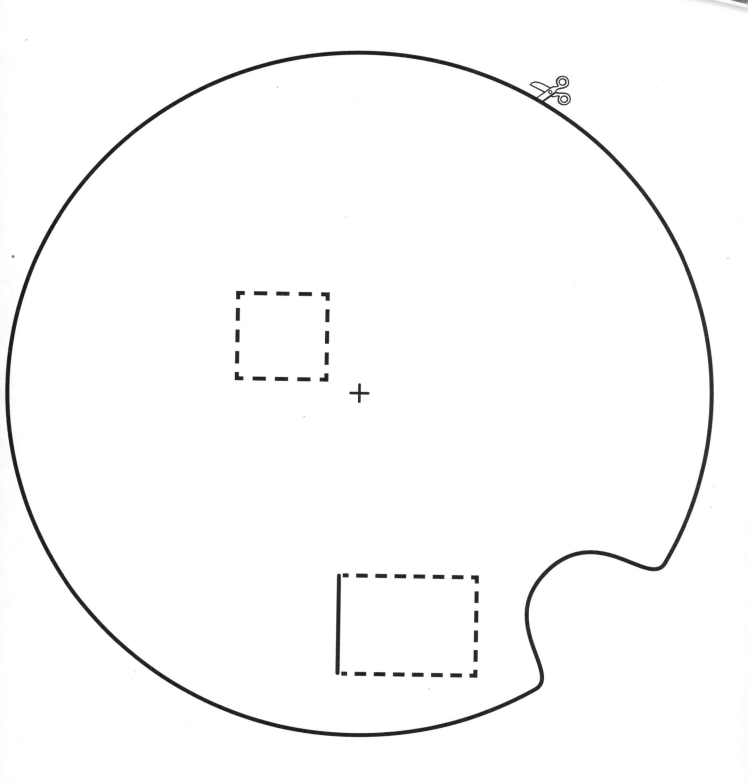